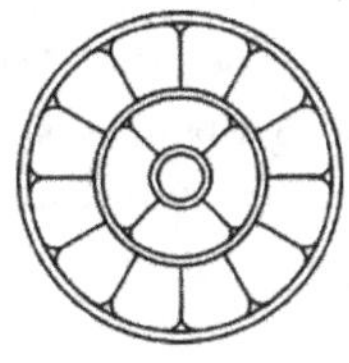 

Eternal Youth

Rays of Light

from

THE MOTHER

ARKA

Auroville

ACKNOWLEDGEMENTS
All quotations and photographs of the Mother and Sri Aurobindo are
copyright of the Sri Aurobindo Ashram Trust, Pondicherry, reproduced here
with acknowledgements and thanks to the Trustees.

Eternal Youth
Copyright : Prisma
Author : Franz Fassbender

ISBN 978-93-95460-71-2 (Paperback)
ISBN 978-93-95460-42-2 (ebook)

BISAC Code:
OCC000000, BODY, MIND & SPIRIT / General
PHI034000, PHILOSOPHY / Social
EDU042000, EDUCATION / Essays

Thema Subject Category:
JBCC9, History of ideas
Q, Philosophy and Religion
QRA, Religion: general

Cataloging-in-Publication Data for this title is available from the
Library of Congress.

Published by:
PRISMA, an imprint of Digital Media Initiatives
PRISMA, Aurelec / Prayogshala,
Auroville 605101, Tamil Nadu, India
www.prisma.haus

Auroville sera le lieu de l'éducation perpétuelle, du progrès constant et d'une jeunesse qui ne vieillit point.

— La Mère

Auroville will be the place of an unending education, of constant progress, and a youth that never ages.

— The Mother

Contents

THE SECRET OF ETERNAL YOUTH

To know how to be reborn into a new life at every moment is the secret of eternal youth.[1]

*

To be young is to live in the future.
To be young is to be always ready to give up what we are in order to become what we must be.
To be young is never to accept the irreparable.[2]

*

Age exists only for those who choose to become old.[3]

*

If one can smile eternally, one is eternally young.[4]

*

Eternal youth: it is a gift the Divine gives us when we unite ourselves with Him.[5]

*

If the growth of consciousness were considered as the principal goal of life, many difficulties would find their solution.

The best way of not becoming old is to make progress the goal of our life.[6]

*
* *

YOUTH IS PERPETUAL PROGRESS

Remain young, never stop striving towards perfection.[1]

*

There is an old age much more dangerous and much more real than the amassing of years: the incapacity to grow and progress.

As soon as you stop advancing, as soon as you stop progressing, as soon as you cease to better yourself, cease to gain and grow, cease to transform yourself, you truly become old, that is to say, you go downhill towards disintegration.

There are young people who are old and there are old people who are young. If you carry in you this flame for progress and transformation, if you are ready to leave everything behind so that you may advance with an alert step, if you are always open to a new progress, a new improvement, a new transformation, then you are eternally young. But if you sit back satisfied with what has been accomplished, if you have the feeling that you have reached your goal and you have nothing left to do but enjoy the fruit of your efforts, then already more than half your body is in the tomb; it is decrepitude and the true death.

Everything that has been done is always nothing compared to what remains to be done.

Do not look behind. Look ahead, always ahead and go forward always.[2]

*

For a happy and effective life, the essentials are sincerity, humility, perseverance and an insatiable thirst for progress. Above all, one must be convinced of a limitless possibility of progress. Progress is youth; at a hundred years of age one can be young.[3]

*

Youth does not depend on the small number of years one has lived, but on the capacity to grow and progress. To grow is to increase one's potentialities, one's capacities; to progress is to make constantly more perfect the capacities that one already possess. Old age does not come from a great number of years but from the incapacity or the refusal to continue to grow and progress. I have known old people of twenty and young people of seventy. As soon as one wants to settle down in life and reap the benefits of one's past efforts, as soon as one thinks that one has done what one had to do and accomplished what one had to accomplish, in short, as soon as one ceases to progress, to advance along the road of perfection, one is sure to fall back and become old.[4]

*

When, on the contrary, you are convinced that what you know is nothing compared to all that remains to be known, when you feel that what you have done is just the starting-point of what remains to be done, when you see the future like an attractive sun shining with the innumerable possibilities yet to be achieved, then you are young, however many are the years you have passed upon earth, young and rich with all the realisations of tomorrow.

And if you do not want your body to fail you, avoid wasting your energies in useless agitation. Whatever you do, do it in a quiet and composed poise. In peace and silence is the greatest strength.[5]

*

Only those years that are passed uselessly make you grow old.

A year spent uselessly is a year during which no progress has been accomplished, no growth in consciousness has been achieved, no further step has been taken towards perfection.

Consecrate your life to the realisation of something higher and broader than yourself and you will never feel the weight of the passing years.[6]

*

How many times in life does one meet people who become pacifists because they are afraid to fight, who long for rest before they have earned it, who are satisfied with a little progress and in their imagination and desires make it into a marvellous realisation so as to justify their stopping half-way.

In ordinary life, already, this happens so much. Indeed,

this is the bourgeois ideal, which had deadened mankind and made man into what he is now: "Work while you are young, accumulate wealth, honour, position; be provident, have a little foresight, put something by, lay up a capital, become an official — so that later when you are forty you `can sit down', enjoy your income and later your pension and, as they say, enjoy a well-earned rest." — To sit down, to stop on the way, not to move forward, to go to sleep, to go downhill towards the grave before one's time, cease to live the purpose of life — to sit down!

The minute one stops going forward, one falls back. The moment one is satisfied and no longer aspires, one begins to die. Life is movement, it is effort, it is a march forward, the scaling of a mountain, the climb towards new revelations, towards future realisations. Nothing is more dangerous than wanting to rest. It is in action, in effort, in the march forward that repose must be found, the true repose of complete trust in the divine Grace, of the absence of desires, of victory over egoism.

True repose comes from the widening, the universalisation of the consciousness. Become as vast as the world and you will always be at rest. In the thick of action, in the very midst of the battle, the effort, you will know the repose of infinity and eternity.[7]

*

One is always in too great a hurry, one wants it to be over very quickly. When one has made an effort, "Oh! well, I made an effort, now I should get the reward of my effort."

In fact, it is because there is not that joy of progress. The joy of progress imagines that even if you have realised the goal you have put before you — take the goal we have in view: if we realise the supramental life, the supramental consciousness — well, this joy of progress says, "Oh! but this will be only a stage in the eternity of time. After this there will be something else, and then after that another and yet another, and always one will have to go further." And that is what fills you with joy. While the idea, "Ah! now I can sit down, it is finished, I have realised my goal, I am going to enjoy what I have done", oh, how dull it is! Immediately one becomes old and stunted.

The definition of youth: we can say that youth is constant growth and perpetual progress — and the growth of capacities, possibilities, of the field of action and range of consciousness, and progress in the working out of details.[8]

*

From the moment you are satisfied and aspire no longer, you begin to die. Life is movement, life is effort; it is marching forward, climbing towards future revelations and realisations. Nothing is more dangerous than wanting to rest.[9]

*

For those who want always to progress, there are three major ways of progressing:

1) To widen the field of one's consciousness.
2) To understand ever better and more completely what one knows.
3) To find the Divine and surrender more and more to his Will.

In other words, this means:

1) To constantly enrich the possibilities of the instrument.

2) To ceaselessly perfect the functioning of this instrument.

3) To make this instrument increasingly receptive and obedient to the Divine.

To learn to understand and do more and more things. To purify oneself of all that prevents one from being totally surrendered to the Divine. To make one's consciousness more and more receptive to the Divine Influence.

One could say: to widen oneself more and more, to deepen oneself more and more, to surrender oneself more and more completely.[10]

*

Openness is the will to receive and to utilise for progress the force and influence; the constant aspiration to remain in touch with the Consciousness; the faith that the force and consciousness are always with you, around you, inside you and that you have only to let nothing stand in the way of your receiving them.[11]

*

One must have an unvarying will to acquire what one does not have in one's nature, to know what one does not yet know, to be able to do what one cannot yet do.

One must progress constantly in the light and the peace which come from the absence of personal desire.[12]

*

Even the most beautiful thoughts will not make us progress unless we have a constant will for them to be expressed in us through nobler feelings, more exact sensations and better actions.[13]

*

Progress: to be ready, at every minute, to give up all one is and all one has in order to advance on the way.[14]

*

Each new dawn brings the possibility of a new progress.

We move forward without haste, for we are sure of the future.[15]

*

*   *

THE CAUSES OF AGING

T he coming of old age is due to two suggestions. First, the general collective suggestion — people telling you that you are getting old and can't do one thing or another. There is also the individual suggestion which keeps repeating, "I am getting old, I mustn't attempt this or that."

The truth is quite different. Before thirty, the energy goes out in a spendthrift way because of the play of impulses. After thirty, there is a settling down and one is expected to have a plenitude of energy. At fifty, blossoming begins. At eighty, one becomes capable of full production.[1]

*

Some quite interesting discoveries are being made: that the cell is immortal, and that aging results merely from a combination of circumstances. This research is tending towards the conclusion that aging is merely a bad habit — which seems to be true...

And this is just what I am realising (I don't think it is anything unique or exceptional): the closer one draws to

the cell itself, the more the cell says, "But I am immortal!"
Only it must become conscious. But this takes place almost
automatically: the brain cells are very conscious; the cells of
the hands and arms of musicians are very conscious; with
athletes and gymnasts, the cells of the entire body are won-
derfully conscious. So, being conscious, those cells become
conscious of their principle of immortality and say, "Why
would I want to grow old? Why!" They don't want to grow
old. It is very interesting.[2]

*

People's ordinary consciousness (it is not a question of
ideas, concepts or anything of that kind: it is the body's
consciousness, the consciousness of the body's cells), the
ordinary, natural, normal consciousness is a consciousness
full of grating and friction, in perpetual disorder, and that
is the cause of aging...

But the other way is a sort of harmonious, undulating
movement (gesture of big waves), almost beyond time, not
quite: there is some sort of time sense, but secondary, somewhat in the distance. And this movement (same gesture)
gives a sense of eternity — of everlastingness, at any rate
— there is no reason for it to cease. There is no friction, no
conflict, no wear and tear, it can go on indefinitely.[3]

*

From the viewpoint of spiritual knowledge, decrepitude and decay — disintegration — are quite simply and
undoubtedly the result of a wrong attitude.[4]

*

The effect of the ego... is to shrivel the being. It is the cause of aging, it dries you up — the being shrivels under it like a withering flower.[5]

*

Concentration upon oneself means decay and death. Concentration on the Divine alone brings life and growth and realisation.[6]

*
* *

THE NECESSITY OF DEATH

*W**hy are men obliged to leave their bodies?*

Because they do not know how to keep up with Nature in her progress towards the Divine.[1]

*

There is now abroad the beginning of a knowledge among the scientists that death is not a necessity. But the whole of humanity believes firmly in death; it is, one might say, a general human suggestion based on a long unchanging experience. If this belief could be cast out first from the conscious mind, then from the vital nature and the subconscious physical layers, death would no longer be inevitable...

It was the conditions of matter upon earth that made death indispensable. The whole sense of the evolution of matter has been a growth from a first state of unconsciousness to an increasing consciousness. And in this process of growth dissolution of forms became an inevitable necessity, as things actually took place. For a fixed form was needed in order that the organised individual consciousness might have a stable support. And yet it is the fixity of the form that made death inevitable... The individual form persisted as a too binding mould; it cannot follow the movements of the forces; it cannot change in harmony with the progressive change in the universal dynamism; it cannot meet continually Nature's demand or keep pace with her; it gets out of the current. At a certain point of this growing disparity and disharmony between the form and the force that presses upon it, a complete dissolution of the form is unavoidable. A new form must be created, a new harmony and purity made possible. This is the true significance of death and this is its use in Nature. But if the form can become more quick and pliant and the cells of the body can be awakened to change with the changing consciousness, there would be no need of a drastic dissolution, death would be no longer inevitable.[2]

*

One year added to another need not bring a deterioration. It is only a habit of Nature. It is only a habit of what is happening at this moment. And that is exactly the cause of death. One can foresee quite well, on the contrary, that the movement for perfection which is at the beginning of life might continue under another form...

One could have a body that grows from perfection to perfection. There are many things in the body that make you say: "Ah, if it were like that! Ah, I would like it to be thus!" (I am not speaking of your character, for there are so many things that need changing; I am speaking only of your physical appearance.) You see some disharmony somewhere and you say: "If this disharmony disappeared, how much better would it be!"... But why don't you think that it could be done? If you look at yourself in quite an objective way — not with that sort of attachment one has for one's little person, but quite objectively, you look at yourself as you would look at another person and tell yourself: "But this thing is not altogether in harmony with that", and if you look yet more closely, it becomes very interesting: you discover that this disharmony is the expression of a defect in your character. It is because in your character there is something a bit twisted, not quite harmonious, and in your body this is reproduced somewhere. You try to arrange it in your body and you find out that to get back to the source of this physical disharmony, you have to find out the defect in your inner being. And then you begin to work and the result is obtained.

You don't know to what an extent the body is plastic! From another standpoint, I would say it is terribly rigid and that is why the body deteriorates. But that is because we do not know how to make use of it. We do not know, when we are still fresh like little leaves, how to will for a luxuriant, magnificent, faultless flowering. And instead of telling oneself with a somewhat miserable look: "It is a pity my arms are too thin or my legs are too long or my back is not straight or my head is not quite harmonious", if one said: "It must be otherwise, my arms must be proportionate, my body harmonious, every form in me must express a higher beauty", then one would succeed. And you will succeed if you know how to do it with the true will that is persistent, tranquil, that is not impatient, does not care for appearances of defeat, continues its work quietly, very quietly, continues to will that it be so, to look for the inner reason, to discover it, to work with energy. Immediately, as soon as you see a little black worm somewhere, which does not look pretty and makes a small rather unpleasant, disgusting stain, you pick it up, pull it out and throw it away and put a lovely light in its place. And after a time you discover: "Why! that disharmony I had in my face is disappearing; that sign of brutality, unconsciousness which was in my expression, it is going away." And then ten years later you don't recognise yourself any longer...

If the body is to last, it must not deteriorate. There must not be any decay. It must win on one side: it must be a transformation, it must not be a decay. With decay there is no possibility of immortality.[3]

*

Expect nothing from death. Life is your salvation.

It is in life that you must transform yourself. It is upon earth that you progress and it is upon earth that you realise. It is in the body that you win the Victory.[4]

*

If nothing, absolutely nothing in you consents to die, you will not die. For someone to die, there is always a second, perhaps the hundredth part of a second when he gives his consent. If there is not this second of consent, he does not die.

I knew people who should have really died according to all physical and vital laws; and they refused. They said: "No, I will not die", and they lived. There are others who do not need at all to die, but they are of that kind and say: "Ah! Well! Yes, so much the better, it will be finished", and it is finished. Even that much, even nothing more than that: you need not have a persistent wish, you have only to say: "Well, yes, I have had enough!" and it is finished. So it is truly like that. As you say, you may have death standing by your bedside and tell him: "I do not want you, go away", and it will be obliged to go away. But usually one gives

22

way, for one must struggle, one must be strong, one must be very courageous and enduring, must have a great faith in the necessity of life; like someone, for example, who feels very strongly that he has still something to do and he must absolutely do it. But who is sure he has not within him the least bit of a defeatist, somewhere, who just yields and says: "It is all right"?... It is here, the necessity of unifying oneself.

Whatever the way we follow, the subject we study, we always arrive at the same result. The most important thing for an individual is to unify himself around his divine centre; in that way he becomes a true individual, master of himself and his destiny. Otherwise, he is a plaything of forces that toss him about like a piece of cork on a river. He goes where he does not want to go, he is made to do things he does not want to do, and finally he loses himself in a hole without having any strength to recover. But if you are consciously organised, unified around the divine centre, ruled and directed by it, you are master of your destiny. That is worth the trouble of attempting.[5]

*

You have said: "One can neither hasten nor delay its hour." But death comes if one stops progressing. So, if one progresses, one can put off the hour. Or does this mean that from one's birth the day and the moment of death are predestined?

No. This is altogether something else and on another plane. I have written elsewhere that one dies only when one consents to die — which seems to contradict what I have said here... There are two points of view. Here I have taken quite an ordinary, material point of view, that of the physical consciousness. But I have explained somewhere that there are, as it were, different "layers of determinism" in our being. The physical existence has a determinism; the vital existence has a determinism; the mental existence has a determinism; the higher mental, the psychic have a determinism. And then the higher existences have determinisms — the supramental existence has a determinism. And the determinism of everyone comes from the combination of all these determinisms... If, for instance, at a given moment, when the entire physical determinism must necessarily bring death, you suddenly enter into contact with an extremely high determinism, like the supramental one, for example, and you succeed in joining the two, you change your physical determinism completely at that moment: death which had been determined by the physical determinism is abolished, and the conditions change and are pushed back...

It is a very few who are capable of bringing down another determinism into the physical determinism. These can change the hour of death... The power lies in bringing down a higher consciousness into the material consciousness, and with the higher consciousness bringing down a higher determinism which changes the material determinism. And not many have that power. I have said a very few do. In fact it is a very, very few.[6]

*

If one must for some reason or other leave one's body and take a new one, is it not better to make of one's death something magnificent, joyful, enthusiastic, than to make it a disgusting defeat? Those who cling on, who try by every possible means to delay the end even by a minute or two, who give you an example of frightful anguish, show that they are not conscious of their soul... After all, it is perhaps a means, isn't it? One can change this accident into a means; if one is conscious one can make a beautiful thing of it, a very beautiful thing, as of everything. And note, those who do not fear it, who are not anxious, who can die without any sordidness are those who never think about it, who are not haunted all the time by this "horror" facing them which they must escape and which they try to push as far away from them as they can. These, when the occasion comes, can lift their head, smile and say, "Here I am."

It is they who have the will to make the best possible use of their life, it is they who say, "I shall remain here as long as it is necessary, to the last second, and I shall not lose one moment to realise my goal"; these, when the necessity comes, put up the best show. Why? — It is very simple, because they live in their ideal, the truth of their ideal; because that is the real thing for them, the very reason of their being, and in all things they can see this ideal, this reason of existence, and never do they come down into the sordidness of material life.

So, the conclusion:

> One must never wish for death.
> One must never will to die.
> One must never be afraid to die.
> And in all circumstances one must will to exceed oneself.[7]

*

There is not so much difference between what men call "life" and what they call "death": the difference is very small, and when you go to the bottom of the problem in all its details, the difference is even smaller. People always make a clean cut between the two — that is quite stupid:

there are living people who are half dead and there are many dead people who are VERY much alive.[8]

*

But people are so ignorant! They make such a fuss over death, as if it were the end — this word "death" is so absurd! I see it as simply passing from one house into another or from one room to another; you take one simple step, you cross the threshold, and there you are on the other side — and then you come back...

And when you live in your soul there is a continuity, because the soul remembers, it keeps the whole memory; it remembers all occurrences, even outer occurrences, all the outer movements it has been associated with. So it is a continuous, uninterrupted movement, here and there, from one room to another, from one house to another, from one life to another.[9]

*

Before being able to reach the condition in which death isn't necessary, you absolutely have to find it... entirely natural, an unimportant event. It is that, above all, something that has very little importance. [10]

*

*   *

THE MIND, VITAL AND PHYSICAL
IN AGING

The physical being, in the state in which it is at present — well, having reached a certain point of ascent, it comes down again. There are elements which may not come down again grossly; but still it does come down, one can't deny it.

The vital being — not necessarily, nor the mental being. The vital being, if it knows how to get connected with the universal force, can very easily have no retrogression; it can continue to ascend. And the mental being, it is absolutely certain, is completely free from all degeneration if it continues to develop normally. So these always make progress so long as they remain co-ordinated and under the influence of the psychic.

It is only the physical being which grows and decomposes. But this comes from its lack of plasticity and receptivity and by its very nature; it is not inevitable. Therefore there is room to think that at a given moment, as the physical consciousness itself progresses consciously and deliberately, well, to a certain extent and increasingly the body itself will be able, first to resist decay — which, obviously, must be the first movement — and then gradually begin to grow in inner perfection till it overcomes the forces of decomposition.

But truly speaking, it is the only thing which for the moment does not progress. Everything else is progressing.

But this substance itself — that is, this material physical substance which forms it constitutes an organism which lives for a certain length of time in a given form and then this form declines and dissolves — the substance itself constituting these successive forms progresses through all these forms. That is, the molecular, cellular substance — perhaps even the cellular — the molecular and atomic, is progressing in its capacity to express the divine Force and Consciousness. Through all these organisms this substance becomes more and more conscious, more and more luminous, more and more receptive, until it reaches a perfection sufficient for it to become a possible vehicle for the divine Force itself which will be able to use it as it uses the elements of the other parts of the creation, like the mind or the vital.

And at that moment the physical substance will be ready to manifest in the world the new Consciousness, new Light, new Will. Through all the centuries, through countless lives, passing through innumerable organisms, using countless experiences it, so to speak, becomes refined; it is prepared, and becomes more and more receptive and open to the divine Forces.[1]

*

All who create mentally, study and live in mental activity, if the mental activity is constant, can progress indefinitely. Mind in the human being does not stop functioning even when the physical instrument has deteriorated. It may no longer manifest its intelligence materially, if there is a lesion in the brain, for example, but the mind itself, independently of the instrument, nothing can prevent from progressing, from continuing to grow. It is a being that lasts infinitely longer than the physical. It is still young when physically one is already old. Only when you do not take enough care to keep your brain in a good state, only if accidents occur and there are lesions then you can no longer express yourself. But the mind in itself continues to grow. And those who have a sufficient physical balance, for example, those who have not gone to excesses of any kind, who have never maltreated their body, who have never poisoned themselves like most people — who have never smoked, drunk alcohol and so on — keep their brain in a relatively good condition and they can progress, even in their expression, till the end of their life. It is only if in the last years of their life they make a kind of withdrawal within themselves, that they lose their power of expression. But the mind goes on progressing.[2]

*

To learn constantly, not just intellectually but psychologically, to progress in regard to character, to cultivate our qualities and correct our defects, so that everything may be an opportunity to cure ourselves of ignorance and incapacity — then life becomes tremendously interesting and worth living.[3]

*

One can also teach the body that there is almost no limit to its growth in capacities or its progress, provided that one discovers the true method and the right conditioning. This is one of the many experiments which we want to attempt in order to break these collective suggestions and show the world that human potentialities exceed all imagination.[4]

*

When the body has learned the art of constantly progressing towards an increasing perfection, we shall be well on the way to overcoming the inevitability of death.[5]

*

It is good to do exercises and to lead a simple and hygienic life, but for the body to be truly perfect, it must open to the divine forces, it must be subject only to the divine influence, it must aspire constantly to realise the Divine.[6]

*

* *

AWAKENING CONSCIOUSNESS IN MATTER

"Death is the question Nature puts continually to Life
and her reminder to it that it has not yet found itself.
If there were no siege of death, the creature would
be bound forever in the form of an imperfect living.
Pursued by death he awakes to the idea of perfect life
and seeks out its means and its possibilities."
(Sri Aurobindo, SABCL, 16:386)

...This is a question which every person whose consciousness is awakened a little has asked himself at least once in his life. There is in the depths of the being such a need to perpetuate, to prolong, to develop life, that the moment one has a first contact with death, which, although it may be quite an accidental contact, is yet inevitable, there is a sort of recoil in the being.

In persons who are sensitive, it produces horror; in others, indignation. There is a tendency to ask oneself: "What is this monstrous farce in which one takes part without wanting to, without understanding it? Why are we born, if it is only to die? Why all this effort for development, progress, the flowering of the faculties, if it is to come to a diminution ending in decline and disintegration?..." Some feel a revolt in them, others less strong feel despair and always this question arises: "If there is a conscious Will behind all that, this Will seems to be monstrous."

But here Sri Aurobindo tells us that this was an indispensable means of awakening in the consciousness of matter the need for perfection, the necessity of progress, that without this catastrophe, all beings would have been satisfied with the condition they were in — perhaps.... This is not certain.

But then, we have to take things as they are and tell ourselves that we must find the way out of it all.

The fact is that everything is in a state of perpetual progressive development, that is, the whole creation, the whole universe is advancing towards a perfection which seems to recede as one goes forward towards it, for what seemed a perfection at a certain moment is no longer perfect after a time. The most subtle states of being in the consciousness follow this progression even as it is going on, and the higher up the scale one goes, the more closely does the rhythm of the advance resemble the rhythm of the universal development, and approach the rhythm of the divine development; but the material world is rigid by nature, transformation is slow, very slow, there, almost imperceptible for the measurement of time as human consciousness perceives it... and so there is a constant disequilibrium between the inner and outer movement, and this lack of balance, this incapacity of the outer forms to follow the movement of the inner progress brings about the necessity of decomposition and the change of forms. But if, into this matter, one could infuse enough consciousness to obtain the same rhythm, if matter could become plastic enough to follow the inner progression, this rupture of balance would not occur, and death would no longer be necessary.

So, according to what Sri Aurobindo tells us, Nature has

found this rather radical means to awaken in the material consciousness the necessary aspiration and plasticity.

It is obvious that the most dominant characteristic of matter is inertia, and that, if there were not this violence, perhaps the individual consciousness would be so inert that rather than change it would accept to live in a perpetual imperfection... That is possible. Anyway, this is how things are made, and for us who know a little more, there is only one thing that remains to be done, it is to change all this, as far as we have the means, by calling the Force, the Consciousness, the new Power which is capable of infusing into material substance the vibration which can transform it, make it plastic, supple, progressive...

Why does this body, as soon as some progress has been made, feel the need to sit down? It is tired. It says, "Oh! you must wait. I must be given time to rest." This is what leads it to death. If it felt within itself that ardour to do always better, become more transparent, more beautiful, more luminous, eternally young, one could escape from this macabre joke of Nature.

For her this is of no importance. She sees the whole, she sees the totality; she sees that nothing is lost, that it is only a recombining of quantities, numberless minute elements, without any importance, which are put back into a pot and mixed well — and something new comes out of it. But that game is not amusing for everybody. And if in one's consciousness one could be as vast as she, more powerful than she, why shouldn't one do the same thing in a better way?

This is the problem which confronts us now. With the addition, the new help of this Force which has descended, which is manifesting, working, why shouldn't one take in hand this tremendous game and make it more beautiful, more harmonious, more true?

It only needs brains powerful enough to receive this Force and formulate the possible course of action. There must be conscious beings powerful enough to convince Nature that there are other methods than hers.... This looks like madness, but all new things have always seemed like madness before they became realities.[1]

*

The first thing the physical consciousness must understand is that all the difficulties we meet with in life come from the fact that we do not rely exclusively on the Divine for the help we need.

The Divine alone can liberate us from the mechanism of universal Nature. And this liberation is indispensable for the birth and development of a new race.

It is only by giving ourselves entirely to the Divine in perfect trust and gratitude that the difficulties will be overcome.[2]

*
*   *

A NEW BIRTH
INTO THE TRUE CONSCIOUSNESS

What is called "new birth" is the birth into the spiritual life, the spiritual consciousness; it is to carry in oneself something of the spirit which, individually, through the soul, can begin to rule the life and be the master of existence.[1]

*

A change of consciousness is equivalent to a new birth, a birth into a higher sphere of existence.[2]

*

New birth: the birth of the true consciousness, that of the Divine Presence in us.[3]

*

The only thing that is truly effective is the change of consciousness; it is the inner liberation through an intimate,

constant union, absolute and inevitable, with the vibration
of the supramental forces. The preoccupation of every second, the will of all the elements of the being, the aspiration
of the entire being, including all the cells of the body, is
this union with the supramental forces, the divine forces...
The only thing that matters is the constant, total, complete
contact — constant, yes, constant — with the Force, the
Light, the Truth, the Power, and that ineffable delight of
the supramental consciousness.[4]

*

To sit in meditation before a closed door, as though it
were a heavy door of bronze — and one sits in front of it
with the will that it may open — and to pass to the other
side; and so the whole concentration, the whole aspiration
is gathered into a beam and pushes, pushes, pushes against
this door, and pushes more and more with an increasing
energy until all of a sudden it bursts open, and one en-
ters. It makes a very powerful impression. And so one is
as though plunged into the light and then one has the full
enjoyment of a sudden and radical change of consciousness, with an illumination that captures one entirely, and
the feeling that one is becoming another person. And this
is a very concrete and very powerful way of entering into
contact with one's psychic being.[5]

*
* *

TOWARDS IMMORTALITY

Life is immortal. It is only the body that dissolves.[1]

*

If we go a little way within ourselves, we shall discover that there is in each of us a consciousness that has been living throughout the ages and manifesting in a multitude of forms.[2]

*

The figure 100 in itself has no special significance for the length of a human life. But simply because human life has become so complex, it has also become relatively short, and it is now rare to live to be a hundred.

When man lived in harmony with Nature, his life lasted longer.

When man lives by and for the Divine, his life will be longer, and one day the Divine will reveal to him the secret of immortality.[3]

*

Long ago there were people who came here because they thought that joining the Ashram was sufficient to make one immortal. And they aspired much for immortality. Naturally, they were old people who did not see a very long road before them and desired to extend it indefinitely — for that is what men understand by "immortality", an indefinite prolongation of what they are. So, to the first person who made this remark, I replied, "I do not know if everyone can become immortal — probably not — but even among those who have the capacity of becoming immortal, how many are ready to pay the price for it?" Because the number of things which have to be left behind is so considerable that perhaps half-way they would say, "Ah, no, the price is too much."...

There were many people, a very large number, who asked me what the new life would be like and to whom I said, "There will be an interchange of forces, a circulating energy; the structure of the body will be quite different, all these ungainly organs will disappear and be replaced by psychological functions; and the necessity of eating, always eating, will disappear."... I saw faces getting longer and longer! People said, "Oh! and all the good things we eat, all that will go?"

These are small instances, there are many others, things more important. The most important, the most difficult thing is to renounce one's ego, for to somebody who is not ready, to renounce his ego is like dying and dying much more than a physical death, for to him the death of the ego is like a dissolution of the being — this is not correct but it begins by giving this sort of impression. To be immortal one must renounce all limitations and the ego is the greatest of limitations; hence if "I" am not immortal, what is the good of that?[4]

*

If you want your physical consciousness to be in a state which admits of physical immortality, you must be free to such an extent from everything which at present represents the physical consciousness that it becomes at every second a battle. All feelings, all sensations, all thoughts, all reflexes, all attractions, all repulsions, all existing things, all that forms the fabric of our physical life must be overcome, transformed and freed from all their habits. This is a battle of every second against thousands and millions of enemies. Unless you feel you are a hero, it is better not to try.[5]

*

The first battle to be fought is already formidable: it is the mental battle against a collective suggestion that is massive, overwhelming, compelling, a suggestion based on thousands of years of experience, on a law of Nature that does not yet seem to have had any exception. It translates itself into this stubborn assertion: it has always been so, it cannot be any different; death is inevitable and it is madness to hope that it can be anything else. The concert is unanimous and till now even the most advanced scientist has hardly dared to sound a discordant note, a hope for the future. As for the religions, most of them have based their power of action on the fact of death and they assert that God wanted man to die since he created him mortal. Many of them make death a deliverance, a liberation, sometimes even a reward. Their injunction is: submit to the will of the Highest, accept without revolt the idea of death and you shall have peace and happiness. In spite of all this, the mind must remain unshakable in its conviction and sustain an unbending will. But for one who has resolved to conquer death, all these suggestions have no effect and cannot affect his certitude which is based on a profound revelation.

The second battle is the battle of the feelings, the fight against attachment to everything one has created, everything one has loved. By assiduous labour, sometimes at the cost of great efforts, you have built up a home, a career, a social, literary, artistic, scientific or political work, you have formed an environment with yourself at the centre and you depend on it at least as much as it depends on you. You are surrounded by a group of people, relatives, friends, helpers, and when you think of your life, they occupy almost as great a place as yourself in your thought, so much so that if they were to be suddenly taken away from you, you would feel lost, as if a very important part of your being had disappeared.

It is not a matter of giving up all these things, since they make up, at least to a great extent, the aim and purpose of your existence. But you must give up all attachment to these things, so that you may feel capable of living without them, or rather so that you may be ready, if they leave you, to rebuild a new life for yourself, in new circumstances, and to do this indefinitely, for such is the consequence of immortality. This state may be defined in this way: to be able to organise and carry out everything with utmost care and attention and yet remain free from all desire and attachment, for if you wish to escape death, you must not be bound by anything that will perish.

After the feelings come the sensations. Here the fight is pitiless and the adversaries formidable. They can sense the slightest weakness and strike where you are defenceless. The victories you win are only fleeting and the same battles are repeated indefinitely. The enemy whom you thought you had defeated rises up again and again to strike you. You must have a strongly tempered character, an untiring endurance to be able to withstand every defeat, every rebuff, every denial, every discouragement and the immense weariness of finding yourself always in contradiction with daily experience and earthly events.

We come now to the most terrible battle of all, the physical battle which is fought in the body; for it goes on without respite or truce. It begins at birth and can end only with the defeat of one of the two combatants: the force of transformation and the force of disintegration. I say at birth, for in fact the two movements are in conflict from the very moment one comes into the world, although the conflict becomes conscious and deliberate only much later. For every indisposition, every illness, every malformation, even accidents, are the result of the action of the force of disintegration, just as growth, harmonious development, resistance to attack, recovery from illness, every return to the normal functioning, every progressive improvement, are due to the action of the force of transformation. Later on, with the development of the consciousness, when the fight becomes deliberate, it changes into a frantic race between the two opposite and rival movements, a race to see which one will reach its goal first, transformation or death. This means a ceaseless effort, a constant concentration to call down the regenerating force and to increase the receptivity of the cells to this force, to fight step by step, from point to point against the devastating action of the forces of destruction and decline, to tear out of its grasp everything that is capable of responding to the ascending urge, to enlighten, purify and stabilize. It is an obscure and obstinate struggle, most often without any apparent result or any external sign of the partial victories that have been won and are ever uncertain — for the work that has been done always seems to need to be redone; each step forward is most often made at the cost of a setback elsewhere and what has been done one day can be undone the next. Indeed, the victory can be sure and lasting only when it is total. And all that takes time, much time, and the years pass by inexorably, increasing the strength of the adverse forces.

All this time the consciousness stands like a sentinel in a trench: you must hold on, hold on at all costs, without a quiver of fear or a slackening of vigilance, keeping an unshakable faith in the mission to be accomplished and in the help from above which inspires and sustains you. For the victory will go to the most enduring.[6]

*

What is lasting, eternal, immortal and infinite, that indeed is worth having, worth conquering, worth possessing. It is divine Light, divine Love, divine Life — it is also Supreme Peace, Perfect Joy and All-Mastery upon earth with the Complete Manifestation as the crowning.[7]

*

*   *

REFERENCES

The texts for this compilation have been selected from the following works of the Mother: *Collected Works of the Mother* (**CWM**) 1972-80, Volume 3, 4, 5, 6, 7, 8, 9, 12, 14, 15,16, published by the Sri Aurobindo Ashram; *Mother's Agenda* (**AG**), translated and rendered in English, under the direction of Satprem, between 1979 and 1983, by the Institut de Recherches Evolutives, Paris and Mira Aditi Center Mysore, India, and from *Mother India* (**MI**).

The Secret of Eternal Youth
1   **CWM** 12:122
2   **Ibid.**   12:120
3   **Ibid.**   12:271
4   **Ibid.**   14:190
5   **Ibid.**   15:124
6   **Ibid.**   12:123

Youth is Perpetual Progress
1   **CWM** 15:188
2   **Ibid.**   3:238
3   **Ibid.**   12:121
4   **Ibid.**   12:257
5   **Ibid.**   12:121
6   **Ibid.**   12:120
7   **Ibid.**   9:65
8   **Ibid.**   8:20
9   **Ibid.**   15:82
10   **Ibid.**   16:433-434
11   **Ibid.**   14:151
12   **Ibid.**   14:167
13   **Ibid.**   14:167

14 **Ibid**. 15:82
15 **Ibid**. 15:81

Causes of Aging
1 **MI,** May 1963, p.5
2 **AG** 16.10.1962, p. 384
3 **AG** 23.02.1963, p. 58
4 **CWM** 15:131
5 **AG**   2.10.1961, p. 341
6 **CWM** 14:14-15

The Necessity of Death
1 **CWM** 15:131
2 **Ibid**.   3:36-37
3 **Ibid**.   5:112-116 passim
4 **Ibid**.   3:198
5 **Ibid**.   5:138-39
6 **Ibid**.   6:47-52 passim
7 **Ibid**.   4:355-356
8 **AG** 4.10.1967, p. 326
9 **Ibid**. 24.06.1961, p. 237-38
10 **Ibid**. 26.06.1968, p. 179

The Mind, Vital and Physical in Aging
1 **CWM**   7:425-426
2 **Ibid**.   5:210-211
3 **Ibid**.   16:430
4 **Ibid**.   12:257
5 **Ibid**.   16:429
6 **Ibid**.   15:147

Awakening Consciousness in Matter
1 **CWM**   9:33-36 passim
2 **Ibid**.   16: 431

A New Birth into the True Consciousness
1 **CWM**   9:431
2 **Ibid.**   15:66
3 **Ibid.**   15:241
4 **Ibid.**   9:118-119
5 **Ibid.**   7:272

Towards Immortality
1 **CWM**   15:133
2 **Ibid.**   15:134
3 **Ibid.**   17:378
4 **Ibid.**   4:69-70
5 **Ibid.**   5:318
6 **Ibid.**   12:82-85
7 **Ibid.**   14:8

International Publications

Auroville Architecture
by Franz Fassbender

Auroville Form Style and Design
by Franz Fassbender

Landscapes and Gardens of Auroville
by Franz Fassbender

Inauguration of Auroville
by Franz Fassbender

Auroville in a Nutshell
by Tim Wrey

Death doesn't exist
The Mother on Death, Sri Aurobindo on Rebirth
Compiled by Franz Fassbender

Divine Love
Compiled by Franz Fassbender

Five Dream
by Sri Aurobindo

A Vision
Compiled by Franz Fassbender

Passage to More than India
by Dick Batstone

The Mother on Japan
Compiled by Franz Fassbender

Children of Change: A Spiritual Pilgrimage
by Amrit (Howard Shoji Iriyama)

Memories of Auroville - told by early Aurovilians
by Janet Feran

The Journeying Years
by Dianna Bowler

Auroville Reflected
by Bindu Mohanty

Finding the Psychic Being
by Loretta Shartsis

The Teachings of Flowers
The Life and Work of the Mother of the Sri Aurobindo
Ashram
by Loretta Shartsis

The Supramental Transformation
by Loretta Shartsis

The Mother's Yoga - 1956-1973 (English & French)
Vol. 1, 1956-1967 & Vol. 2, 1968-1973
by Loretta Shartsis

Antithesis of Yoga
by Jocelyn Janaka

Bougainvilleas PROTECTION
by Narad (Richard Eggenberger), Nilisha Mehta

Crossroad The New Humanity
by Paulette Hadnagy

Die Praxis Des Integralen Yoga
by M. P. Pandit

The Way of the Sunlit Path
by William Sullivan

Wildlife great and small of India's Coromandel
by Tim Wrey

A New Education With A Soul
by Marguerite Smithwhite

Featured Titles

Divine Love

The texts presented in this book are selected from the Mother and Sri Aurobindo.

"Awakened to the meaning of my heart. That to feel love and oneness is to live. And this the magic of our golden change, is all the truth I know or seek, O sage."

Sri Aurobindo, Savitri, Book XII, Epilog

A Vision by the Mother

On 28th May 1958, the Mother recounted a vision she once had of a wonderful Being of Love and Consciousness, emanated from the Supreme Origin and projected directly into the Inconscient so that the creation would gradually awaken to the Supramental Consciousness. The Mother's account of this vision was brought out a first time in November 1906, in the Revue Cosmique, a monthly review published in Paris.

A Dream – Aims and Ideals of Auroville
the Mother on Auroville

50 years of Auroville from 28.02.1968 - 28.02.2018

Today, information about Auroville is abundant. Many people try to make meaning out of Auroville – about its conception, to what direction should we grow towards, and, what are we doing here?

But what was Mother's original Dream and what was her Vision for Auroville back then?

Matrimandir Talks by the Mother

This book presents most of Mother's Matrimandir talks, including how she conceived the idea for this special concentration and meditation building in Auroville.

Memories of Auroville - Told by early Aurovilians

Memories of Auroville is a book about the very early days of Auroville based on interviews made in 1997 with Aurovilians who lived here between 1968 and 1973. The interviews presented in this book are part of a history program for newcomers that I had created with my friend, Philip Melville in 1997. The plan was to divide Auroville's history into different eras and then interview Aurovilians according to their area of knowledge. Our first section would cover the years from 1968 till 1973 when the Mother was still in her physical body.

The Way of the Sunlit Path

May The Way of the Sunlit Path be a convenient guide for activating this ancient truth as a support for a Conscious Evolution.
May it illumine the transformation offered to us in the Integral Yoga.

A Dream Takes Shape (in English, French, Hindi)

A comprehensive brochure on the international township of Auroville in, ranging from its Charter and "Why Auroville?" to the plan of the township, the central Matrimandir, the national pavilions and residences, to working groups, the economy, making visits, how to join, its relationship to the Sri Aurobindo Ashram, and its key role in the future of the world. This brochure endeavours to highlight how The Mother envisioned Auroville from its inception, some of the major achievements realised over the years, and some of the difficulties currently faced in implementing the guidelines which she gave.

Mother on Japan

I had everything to learn in Japan. For four years, from an artistic point of view, I lived from wonder to wonder. And everything in this city, in this country, from beginning to end, gives you the impression of impermanence, of the unexpected, the exceptional... ...everything in this city, in this country, from beginning to end, gives you the impression of impermanence, of the unexpected, the exceptional. You always come to things you did not expect; you want to find them again and they are lost – they have made something else which is equally charming.

Auroville Reflected

On 28 February 1968, on an impoverished plateau on the Coromandel Coast of South India, about 4,000 people from around the world gathered for a most unusual inauguration. Handfuls of soil from the countries of the world were mixed together as a symbol of human unity. Why did Indira Gandhi, the erstwhile Prime Minister of India, support this development for "a city the earth needs?" Why did UNESCO endorse this project? Why does the Dalai Lama continue to be involved in the project? What led anthropologist Margaret Mead to insist that records must be kept of its progress? Why did both historian William Irwin Thompson and United Nations representative Robert Muller note that this social experiment may be a breakthrough for humanity even as critics commented, "it is an impossible dream"?

A House For the Third Millennium

Essays on Matrimandir

Nightwatch at the Matrimandir...
A cosmic spectacle; the black expanse above, the big black crater of Matrimandir's excavation carved deep into the soil. The four pillars - two of which are completed and the other two nearing completion - are four huge ships coming together from the four corners of the earth to meet at this pro propitious spot...

Passage to More than India

This book is a voyage of discovery. In 1959 the author, Dick Batstone, a classically educated bookseller in England, with a Christian background, comes across a life of the great Indian polymath Sri Aurobindo, though a series of apparently fortuitous circumstances. A meeting in Durham, England, leads him to a determination to get to the Sri Aurobindo Ashram in Pondicherry, a former French territory south of Madras.